HOUSE PLANTS

ALAN TOOGOOD

Text filmset in Plantin
by Foremost Typesetting Ltd, London

Printed in Belgium by Casterman
ISBN 0 7063 4274 7

ACKNOWLEDGEMENTS

The publishers are grateful to the following agencies for granting
permission to reproduce the following colour photographs: Pat
Brindley (front cover: upper right and lower left; back cover; pp
2, 3, 7, 14, 15, 19, 22, 23, 27, 30, 35 and 38); Harry Smith
Horticultural Photographic Collection (front cover: upper left
and lower right; pp 11, 18, 42 and 47).

Front cover: upper left, *Narcissus* 'Golden Harvest'; upper right,
Hyacinth 'King of the Blues'; lower left, *Euphorbia pulcherrima*
(poinsettia); lower right, *Chlorophytum comosum* (spider plant).

Back cover: *Coleus blumei*

p. 2: *Hippeastrum* 'Apple Blossom' will flower in winter given
adequate warmth.

p. 3: Cinerarias are ideal pot plants for cool rooms.

CONTENTS

CARING FOR HOUSEPLANTS

Your houseplants will grow well and look in the peak of health if you give them the best possible growing conditions and care for them properly. Provided they have adequate light, warmth and humidity, and are correctly watered, fed, cleaned, potted and, if necessary, trimmed, they will amply repay you with a colourful display of flowers or foliage.

LIGHT

It is important to ensure your houseplants receive the right amount of light. Some plants need all the light possible, including some sunshine, while others prefer to grow in subdued light (not direct sunshine) or in shade. I have given light requirements for each of the plants described.

If plants which like plenty of light are grown in shady conditions they will become weak and spindly, the leaves will turn pale and sickly looking and the plants may not produce flowers.

On the other hand, if shade-loving plants are grown in a sunny spot their leaves will become scorched or bleached and look most unsightly.

Most houseplants sold by garden centres and chain stores have pictorial labels which indicate the best growing conditions in respect of light, temperature and so on. Do check these labels before you buy plants to make sure you can provide the right conditions.

The brightest light is to be found immediately in front of the windows and the light is still quite bright at a distance of 60-90 cm (2-3 ft) from the windows. These areas are best reserved for those plants which need very bright light or sunshine.

South-facing windows have full sun for much of the day and can become very hot in the middle of the day during the summer. If the sun is too hot for some plants it can be filtered by means of net curtains. It is best if these can be hung so that

A cool room is needed for *Primula obconica*.

they can be drawn back on dull days so that plants then receive maximum light. Many houseplants are able to take direct winter sun which is very much weaker and so does not cause damage to leaves and flowers.

North-facing windows receive no direct sun but nevertheless the light is very bright and does not fluctuate throughout the day. These are ideal places for foliage houseplants which need very good light.

Further into a room the light intensity will, of course, be much lower, but reflected light from windows is to be recommended and could be achieved by means of mirrors or even light-coloured walls, provided they actually face a window.

The stems and leaves of many houseplants grow towards the source of light – they actually lean over or bend towards the light. This is more pronounced the further into a room a plant is placed. If this happens with some of your plants they should be turned regularly so that all parts receive the same amount of light. Give a quarter turn every few days or so. A word of warning here, though: there are some plants, notably the Christmas cactus, which should not be turned once the flower buds start to appear, otherwise the buds will drop.

TEMPERATURE

I have given suitable temperatures for all the plants described and you will see that there are plants suitable for warm rooms, moderately heated rooms and even very cool rooms. So no part of your house need be devoid of houseplants because temperatures are too low – just choose the right plants and they will thrive.

In general houseplants prefer steady temperatures, with little difference between day and night. In most homes the temperature drops at night when the central heating is turned down or off. However a difference of 5°C (10°F) is perfectly acceptable to most houseplants.

It is not a bad idea to measure the temperature in rooms where you grow houseplants, using a maximum/minimum thermometer which indicates daytime as well as night-time temperatures. This will help you to choose the right plants for your particular rooms.

Avoid placing houseplants near or above radiators, heaters, stoves, etc., for conditions will be far too hot for them and the leaves will become scorched or dried up. However a very wide shelf placed over a radiator will deflect hot air and can make a suitable home for plants which revel in warm dry air, like the sansevieria or mother-in-law's tongue.

Many tropical plants (and this applies to the majority of foliage houseplants) will suffer if they are subjected to very cold conditions. They could well die on you. At all costs avoid leaving plants between the windows and drawn curtains at night during the winter, for in that space it can become extremely cold and plants may be damaged or killed by frost. So make sure you move any plants on the windowsills further into the room before you draw the curtains.

It is essential to avoid subjecting houseplants to cold draughts from windows, doors and so on (although I am not assuming your house is draughty!). Nevertheless if you open the front door on a winter's day you know only too well that you get a rush of cold air into the house. Plants will not be happy with this: they will become chilled and will react by wilting or by dropping leaves and flower buds. Very delicate plants may even die. There are one or two tough houseplants, though, which will tolerate cold draughts.

Incidentally, when you buy plants, say from a chainstore or garden centre, do make sure they are well wrapped up before you take them home otherwise they could become chilled on the journey and then, a few days later, the leaves could drop off.

HUMIDITY

Humidity is the amount of moisture in the air. The majority of our houseplants need moist air around them – some like more humidity than others and this is indicated for each of the plants described. The correct level of humidity (e.g. low, moderate or high) is as important for healthy growth as optimum light and temperature.

It's worth remembering that the warmer a room is kept the drier the air becomes, for the moisture in the air dries up. Warm centrally heated rooms have a very dry atmosphere. In cooler rooms the atmospheric moisture is higher.

Some plants need dry air as they are used to this in the wild, good examples being the desert cacti and succulents. Other plants (the majority) need moist or humid air.

So in warm or moderately heated rooms we must provide humidity for those plants which need it. If we do not provide moist air plants may wilt, the result of a great loss of water through their leaves. Also the leaves may shrivel and die; or leaf tips and edges may turn brown; and leaves and flower buds may drop.

Some warm and moderately heated rooms have higher atmospheric humidity than others due to the way they are used. This can apply to bathrooms and kitchens, so these may be the ideal rooms for some plants which need high humidity, such as the saintpaulias or African violets.

Let us now consider ways of providing humidity for plants. The most popular method is to stand plants in shallow plastic trays filled with a horticultural aggregate (such as Hortag), gravel or shingle. These materials are kept moist so that humid air rises up and around the plants. On no account, though, allow the pots actually to stand in water or the compost will become saturated and plant roots may then rot.

Another idea is to place pots in larger ornamental containers, such as pot holders or troughs and tubs (there must be no drainage holes in these) and the spaces filled with peat or horticultural aggregate, which again is kept moist.

Humidity can also be provided by lightly spraying the leaves of plants with water, using a small mist sprayer. This should be done once or twice a day, depending on the room temperature – the warmer it is the more spraying needed. Never spray plants if the sun is shining on them or it will result in unsightly scorch marks on the leaves and flowers. Don't spray plants with hairy or woolly leaves, but use instead the methods recommended above.

If possible use rainwater for spraying plants if your tapwater is 'hard' (contains lime or chalk) as hard water results in unsightly white chalky deposits on the leaves. These can, however, be sponged off.

The spider plant, *Chlorophytum comosum* 'Variegatum', will flourish in bright light or shade.

WATERING

This aspect of houseplant care can cause problems for beginners who may be uncertain when to water plants and how much water to apply.

However try to get to grips with watering for if you keep plants too wet they could suffer from root rot and die; and if they are not given enough water they will be under great stress and will not grow and flower well.

As a general rule more water is needed in the growing season (spring and summer) than in the rest period (autumn and winter). I have indicated water requirements for each plant described.

So when do we water plants in the growing period? Forget the advice that they should be watered every day, every two days, or whatever. This just does not work out. However bear in mind that most houseplants do not like the compost to dry out too much during this period.

I strongly recommend that you test the compost for moisture with a finger. Press a finger into the compost surface and if it feels dry on top but moist below then give water. If the surface is moist or even wet do not water the plant.

When watering houseplants do not give a 'quick splash' (as so many people do, unfortunately), but fill the space between the compost surface and the rim of the pot with water. This will ensure the compost is moistened right the way down to the bottom of the pot. I have often noticed when buying houseplants that the surface of the compost is right at the top of the pot, with no space for watering. What I generally do then is scrape off some of the compost to provide a space of at least 12 mm (½ in). The alternative is to water from below, by standing the pot almost up to its rim in a bowl of water until the surface of the compost becomes moist. Then remove and allow to drain.

When watering in autumn and winter, during the plants' rest period and when conditions are cooler, watering should be reduced so that the compost is kept only slightly moist. But how do we ensure this?

Again I recommend testing the compost with a finger, pushing it well down into the compost. If the compost is dry on the surface and feels dryish but not completely dry lower down, water can be given, again filling the space between the compost surface and the rim of the pot. Then leave the plant well alone until the compost is drying out again. If in doubt it is far better not to water than to keep the compost too wet. Far better to leave the plant for a few more days, unless it is wilting.

If the compost becomes extremely dry for some reason watering normally with an indoor watering can from above can be futile as the water may simply run off or run straight through the pot without moistening the compost. The solution is to stand the pot in a bowl of water as described above.

There are moisture meters available which you may prefer to use if you feel you cannot rely on the above method of testing for moisture content. They consist of a metal probe which is pushed down into the compost. You read off the state of the compost from a dial at the top, which is marked 'dry', 'moist' and 'wet'.

How can you ensure your houseplants remain moist while you are away for a week or two? If you do not have a kindly friend or neighbour who could look in and water your plants, then you could rig up a simple capillary watering system.

First, obtain a sheet of capillary watering matting from a garden centre (it looks like a sheet of felt). Then cover the kitchen draining board with it, ensuring one end goes well down into the sink. (It's a good idea to moisten the matting thoroughly first). Now stand your houseplants on the matting (on the draining board) after having watered them well. Then fill the sink with water. The plants can now be left, for the matting will remain moist (it draws up water from the sink). The plants will take up the moisture they need from the matting. This system only works for plants which are in plastic pots rather than clay pots.

A final word about watering. Try to collect rainwater as this is far better for houseplants than 'hard' tapwater, although it should be said that the latter will not harm the majority of houseplants.

FEEDING

Houseplants certainly need feeding but do not be too heavy-handed with the fertilizer! For instance, newly potted plants should not be given fertilizer until their roots have grown into the new compost (in practice usually about a couple of months), for there will be sufficient plant foods in the potting compost. Too much fertilizer can be harmful to plants.

Thereafter feeding can be carried out about once a fortnight for most houseplants, but only in the growing season – spring and summer – and perhaps early autumn if plants are still growing vigorously.

Do not feed plants in late autumn, winter or early spring

The Kaffir lily, *Clivia miniata* (BELOW), can be kept for many years. Pot hydrangeas (RIGHT) should be grown in the coolest rooms.

when they are resting, for they will not use the fertilizer and an excess of foods can build up in the compost and damage the roots of the plants.

There are various ways of feeding houseplants but the most popular is to apply a liquid houseplant fertilizer, diluted according to the manufacturer's instructions. There are many proprietary brands available, some being based on seaweed which is rich in plant foods.

Another way of feeding houseplants is to use fertilizer tablets, again specially made for houseplants. These are about the size of an aspirin tablet and are simply pushed into the compost where they release their plant foods over a period of weeks. Very useful if you are inclined to forget to feed your plants, or you do not have much time to feed them.

Plants should not be fed if the compost is dry, so water first if necessary and then feed a few hours later when the plants are fully charged with water.

Finally remember that it is most important to give fertilizers strictly according to the instructions on the bottle or packet, for you could harm plants by applying too much or too strong a solution.

CLEANING

The leaves of houseplants should not be allowed to become covered with dust and grime or they will not function properly and then growth will be poor. So as often as you consider it to be necessary (in most homes this means at least once a month) you should sponge off the leaves with tepid water.

Do not use this method, though, for plants which have hairy or woolley leaves. Instead dust them off with a soft brush.

Any plants with thick shiny leaves, such as the rubber plant, Swiss cheese plant and philodendrons, can, if desired, be treated with a proprietary leaf-shine product to make them even glossier. Some come in aerosol form for easy application. It is essential to follow the manufacturer's instructions on use as leaf-shine products are not suitable for all plants and they could damage others if they are not used correctly.

PRUNING OR TRIMMING

If some of your houseplants such as climbers and rubber plants become too tall, or bare at the base (devoid of leaves) due to old age, do not be afraid to cut them back by as much as half to two-thirds of their height. This generally results in new shoots being produced lower down the stems so the plants become more bushy. The best time of year for this hard cutting back is spring just as the plants are starting into growth after their winter rest.

Some plants 'bleed' milky sap when pruned, particularly rubber plants and their relations, the figs. You should try to stop this by dusting the cuts with powdered charcoal.

Do not be afraid to give other plants a trim, too, if you feel they are becoming leggy or have straggly shoots. For example the shrimp plant needs trimming to keep it neat and bushy. Judiciously reduce the length of the shoots to avoid spoiling the natural shapes of plants. If any plants particularly need pruning I have given details in the plant section.

Sometimes variegated plants (those with green and white or green and yellow leaves) produce the occasional shoot which has all-green leaves. This should be cut out completely otherwise it may take over the plant, for all-green shoots on variegated plants are excessively vigorous.

When pruning or trimming always cut immediately above a growth bud or leaf and use really sharp secateurs to ensure smooth rather than ragged cuts which heal over more quickly. You need only a lightweight pair of secateurs for trimming houseplants.

POTTING

If houseplants are potted on regularly – in other words, moved into larger pots – they will make far better growth and become larger. If plants are allowed to become pot-bound, when the compost is tightly packed with roots, growth will slow down considerably and they will remain on the small side. Also the compost will dry out rapidly so you will be forever watering and there is the risk plants will suffer from lack of moisture. They will also be short of essential foods.

There are a few houseplants, though, which should not be potted on regularly because they have only small root systems and therefore need small pots. The main examples are the urn plant (aechmea), peperomias, foliage begonias, the Christmas cactus and the saintpaulias or African violets.

Avoid potting on in winter when plants are resting for they will not make new roots into the fresh compost and consequently the compost may remain too wet, in which case the roots may rot and the plants will die. The best time to pot on houseplants is in spring just as they are starting into growth.

You must first find out, though, whether or not a plant needs moving into a larger pot by inspecting the roots. To do this turn the pot upside down, tap the rim on the edge of a table to loosen the rootball and slide off the pot. If there is a mass of roots with virtually no compost visible then move on

Peperomia caperata (LEFT), one of the most popular pepper elders. Regal pelargoniums (BELOW) flower freely in early summer and come in various colours.

the plant to a larger pot. If, on the other hand, a large volume of the compost has no roots through it return the plant to the same pot.

Generally plants are potted on to the next size of pot, for example from a 12.5 cm (5 in) pot to a 15 cm (6 in) pot. However more vigorous plants (such as the spider plant or chlorophytum) can with advantage be moved on two sizes – say from a 10 cm (4 in) pot to a 15 cm (6 in) pot.

Plastic pots are generally used for houseplants today but for plants which like very well-drained conditions and dryish compost (such as sansevierias and the desert cacti and succulents) clay pots are recommended. Clays are also best for large specimen plants as they are heavier and more stable so there is less risk of a large plant falling over.

The trend today is to dispense with drainage material in the bottom of the pot. However I do feel that for plants which like very well-drained conditions (such as cacti and succulents) drainage material should be provided. I also consider it necessary when we start using larger pots – say over 15 cm (6 in) in diameter.

The traditional drainage material is broken clay flower pots, known as 'crocks'. A large piece is laid over the drainage hole and then a layer of smaller pieces placed over this. Cover the crocks with a thin layer of coarse peat or leafmould followed by a layer of potting compost which should be firmed.

Now set the plant in the centre of the new pot and fill in with fresh compost, which should also be firmed by using your fingers. You should ensure the top of the rootball is slightly covered with fresh compost and there must be space between the final compost level and the rim of the pot to allow for watering. This can be about 12 mm (½ in) for small pots and up to 2.5 cm (1 in) for large pots.

After potting water in the plants to settle the compost around the roots.

Now let's take a look at composts for houseplants. We have a choice of soil-based potting compost (the traditional John Innes composts) and soilless or peat-based. It is safe to say that virtually all houseplants can be grown in John Innes potting compost. Plants which like very well-drained conditions (such as cacti, succulents and sansevierias) are certainly best grown in JI. I often add some extra grit or coarse sand to make the drainage even better – about one-third extra to a given volume of compost. Some JI mixes you buy can be a bit on the heavy side and pack down solid when they are watered so they remain wet and devoid of air. If you are doubtful about the quality of the JI you buy the addition of extra sand or grit will certainly help to improve it. Also add a little extra peat, which should be moistened before mixing it into the compost.

JI potting compost No. 1 is used for the initial potting of rooted cuttings and seedlings while JI No. 2 is used for potting on, as it contains more fertilizer. Very large plants can be potted into JI No. 3 which is a very rich compost.

Most houseplants will also be happy in the modern soilless or peat-based potting composts. Some are prepared specially for houseplants but the general-purpose brands are just as good. You must use soilless composts according to the instructions on the bags, bearing in mind that they should not be firmed too much or their drainage will be impaired.

You will also find special-purpose composts in garden centres – for example there are composts for cacti and succulents and for plants which do not like lime or chalk in the soil, such as azaleas. These are known as ericaceous composts and will probably be labelled as such.

PESTS AND DISEASES

Yes, even houseplants can be attacked by pests and diseases although they are not so prone as plants in the garden. Keep an eye open for signs of trouble, though.

It is best to use an aerosol houseplant pest killer which will control a wide range of insect pests like greenfly, red spider mites, whitefly, scale insects, mealy bugs and thrips.

If any of your plants become infected with common fungal diseases like mildew (white powdery patches on leaves) and grey mould or botrytis (a greyish rot which affects leaves, stems and flowers of many plants) then take the plants outside and spray them thoroughly with benomyl fungicide. You will need a small hand sprayer for this.

2
INCREASING HOUSEPLANTS

Many houseplants can be propagated, if you want more for yourself or your friends, by taking cuttings of various kinds and by division and plantlets.

STEM CUTTINGS

Many houseplants produce plenty of new side shoots each year and these can be used as cuttings during the spring or summer. Use the tips of the shoots as cuttings making them 5 to 10 cm (2 to 4 in) long. The base of each cutting should be cut cleanly immediately below a leaf joint (where the leaves join the stem). The leaves should be cut off from the lower half of each cutting as near to the stem as possible.

Then dip the bases (the lower 6 mm (¼ in)) of the cuttings in hormone rooting powder to ensure speedy rooting.

Coleus (BELOW) are most attractive as young plants. A variegated form of the popular weeping fig, *Ficus benjamina* (RIGHT).

Insert the cuttings in pots of cutting compost (a mixture of equal parts by volume of peat and coarse sand). Set them around the edge of the pot, up to their lower leaves. Make a hole for each one with a pencil, stand the cutting in it and firm the compost around it with your fingers. Make sure the cuttings are well spaced – they should not be touching each other.

A modern way of rooting cuttings of houseplants is in little transparent pots of clear gel – a clean, easy and efficient method. You will find packs of these in the garden centres.

Root cuttings in a temperature of 18-21°C (65-70°F), either in a small electrically heated window-sill propagating case or direct on a window-sill in a warm room. In the latter instance enclose each pot in a clear polythene bag to ensure humidity. Make sure it is held above the cuttings by inserting a few short thin canes in the pot. Ventilate the cuttings several times a week to allow condensation to disperse.

An indication of rooting is when the tips start into growth (or if you use the transparent pots of gel you will actually see the roots growing). Pot off rooted cuttings into 7.5 cm (3 in) pots.

LEAF CUTTINGS

Some houseplants can be propagated from their leaves in the spring and summer, providing the same rooting conditions as for stem cuttings.

Some plants are increased from whole leaves complete with leaf stalk and examples are peperomias and saintpaulias. Simply insert in pots of cutting compost (or gel) up to the base of the leaf blade. Eventually plantlets will appear at the base of the leaves and then it's time for potting off into small pots.

Begonia rex and *B. masoniana* are also propagated from entire leaves but the leaf stalk is removed. The leaf is then turned upside down and, using a sharp knife or razor blade, the main veins are cut through in a number of places.

Then turn the leaf the right way up and lay it on the surface of a tray of cutting compost. Weight it down with a few small stones so that the cut veins are in close contact with the compost. Plantlets will eventually appear where the veins have been cut through and they should be lifted and potted into small pots.

The sansevieria or mother-in-law's tongue is propagated from sections of leaf but you should bear in mind that, rather surprisingly perhaps, the resultant plants will not have yellow leaf edges like the parent plant.

Remove a complete leaf from your sansevieria and cut it into 5 cm (2 in) long sections, making sure you keep them the right way up. Dip their bases in hormone rooting powder to speed rooting and then insert the sections vertically to half their length in pots of cutting compost or pots of clear gel. When well rooted and plantlets have appeared pot into small pots.

DIVISION

Established houseplants which form clumps of growth, like chlorophytums, ferns, sansevierias and marantas, can be increased by division in the spring just before they start to make new growth.

Remove the plant from its pot and carefully pull the clump apart into a number of portions. If this proves difficult use a sharp knife to cut through matted roots. The outer portions of a clump are younger and therefore more vigorous than the older centre part so these are the parts of the plant to retain. The old centre part can be thrown away. Pot the divisions into pots of a suitable size.

PLANTLETS

There are several houseplants which produce little plants or plantlets and these can be used for propagation. Examples are chlorophytum and tolmiea. The plantlets can be pegged down into small pots of potting compost placed alongside the parent plant. Use a wire peg the shape of a hairpin to hold the plantlet in close contact with the compost. After a few weeks the plantlets will have rooted into their pots and can be cut away from the parent plant to start an independent life.

3
A PLANT FOR EVERY MONTH

There are houseplants, flowering and foliage kinds, to provide colour and interest during each month of the year. Here is a selection of the very best and most popular houseplants with hints on their care and cultivation.

The flowering plants are listed according to a suitable month to buy them, when they will be in flower, although it should be remembered that they will be flowering over several months (on either side of the month under which they are listed).

Foliage houseplants (those with attractive and interesting leaves) can be bought at any time of year for the majority are attractive all the year round. Nevertheless I have still recommended suitable months to buy them. The tropical kinds should ideally be bought in the spring or summer to give them time to become acclimatized to your home before the winter sets in. Then there are the short-term foliage plants (such as coleus) which should be bought when they are at their very best in the summer. Hardier foliage plants can be bought early or late in the year.

JANUARY

Begonia 'Elatior' hybrids (**Winter-flowering Begonia**)
These popular winter-flowering begonias come in a wide range of colours including shades of red, orange, pink and yellow and they bloom over several months. They have fleshy or tuberous roots and in theory can be kept from year to year, but this is not easy and so most people discard them after flowering.

They need a temperature of 16-21°C (60-70°F), but it can drop to 13°C (55°F) at night. Provide moderate humidity and really bright light, but not direct sun. Keep the compost steadily moist as the plants dislike dry roots.

Tough, adaptable mother-in-law's tongue, *Sansevieria trifasciata* 'Laurentii'.

Hippeastrum (Amaryllis, Hippeastrum)

This is a bulb which can be kept for many years. It produces massive trumpet-shaped flowers in shades of red, pink, orange or white. Some consist of two colours.

You can buy bulbs already potted or you can pot your own in autumn. Each large bulb needs a 15 cm (6 in) pot and should be grown in John Innes potting compost No. 1. The upper part of the bulb should be above compost level. Provide a temperature of 16°C (60°F) during the growing season but keep the bulb very cool (but frost free) during its autumn rest period. No extra humidity needed but provide maximum light. Feed fortnightly after flowering. When the leaves die down in late summer/autumn stop watering. Resume early in the year. Repot bulb every four years.

FEBRUARY

Primula (Primroses)

Flowering any time between autumn and late spring, *Primula obconica* and *P. malacoides* (the fairy primrose) have flowers in shades of red, pink, blue, etc. Also recommended is *P.* × *kewensis* with yellow blooms. These plants cannot be kept after flowering so should be discarded.

Keep primulas in a cool room with a temperature between 13 and 16°C (55 and 60°F). Provide a little humidity and maximum light. The compost should be kept moist all the time but don't make the leaves wet. Pick off dead flowers. Some people are allergic to some primulas (*P. obconica* and *P. sinensis*) and come out in a rash if they handle them – a pair of gloves may solve this problem.

Senecio × *hybridus* (Cineraria)

Flowering in winter and spring, the cineraria is a highly popular short-term pot plant with large heads of daisy flowers in many colours, including shades of red, pink and blue.

Keep in a cool room with a temperature of 13-16°C (55-60°F), which can drop to 10°C (50°F) at night. A little humidity is appreciated and really bright light is essential – e.g. a north-facing windowsill. Keep the compost steadily moist and remove dead flowers.

MARCH

Chlorophytum comosum 'Variegatum' (Spider plant)

From now onwards we can start buying foliage plants and to be seen in virtually every home is the tough adaptable spider plant with its green and white striped leaves and little plantlets dangling on the ends of the old flower stalks.

It can be grown in warm or cool rooms but should not be subjected to a temperature lower than 7°C (45°F). It likes high humidity when conditions are warm and really good light, including a little sunshine. The spider plant can also be grown in a shady corner, however. Keep the plant well watered in the growing season but water very sparingly in autumn and winter. Feed fortnightly when in full growth.

Primula (Coloured primroses)

In the shops and garden centres around Mothers' Day we see coloured primroses grown as pot plants. These are varieties of our native primrose but have flowers in various colours, such as shades of red, pink and blue. They can be planted in the garden after flowering.

Keep the plants in a cool room with a temperature between 13 and 16°C (55 and 60°F). Provide a little humidity and maximum light. The compost should be kept moist at all times but keep water off the leaves. Pick off dead flowers to ensure more follow – the plants have a long flowering period.

APRIL

Adiantum raddianum (Maidenhair fern)

Spring is the time for ferns, like the dainty maidenhair fern with its wiry black stems and fan-shaped pale green leaflets. It makes a lovely foil for spring-flowering pot plants like primulas.

It should be grown in a temperature of 16-18°C (60-65°F) at all times and needs high humidity (but do not mist spray the leaves). This fern needs bright light but must not be subjected to direct sun. Keep the compost steadily moist and feed every two weeks in the spring and summer. Only pot on when the plant becomes pot-bound as it does not like too large a pot.

Clivia miniata (Kaffir lily)

This is a flowering plant which can be kept for many years. In the spring, from among strap-shaped leaves, it produces large heads of trumpet-shaped blooms which may be orange or orange-red. They last for many weeks.

Provide a temperature of 16°C (60°F) but during the winter rest period reduce it to 10°C (50°F). A little humidity is appreciated when conditions are warm. Provide really good light and ensure the plant also receives some sunshine. Water well in spring and summer, moderately in autumn, and keep the plant barely moist in winter. In spring and summer feed every two weeks. Pot on the plant when pot-bound, using John Innes potting compost. Cut off the dead flower heads.

Jasminum polyanthum (Jasmine)

An easily grown sweet-smelling climber which has white flowers over a long period in spring. Grow it up canes or wall trellis.

As jasmine is almost hardy grow it in a cool room with a temperature of no more than 16°C (60°F); it can drop to 5°C (40°F) in winter. Provide moderate humidity and mist spray the leaves in summer. The plant must have really good light, including some sunshine, but beware of hot scorching sun.

Pot on the plant after flowering and also prune it at this time by reducing old shoots by half to two-thirds of their

The ornamental pepper, *Capsicum annuum*, holds its berries for many months.

length. The compost must be kept moist for most of the year
but for several weeks after flowering allow it to become fairly
dry to give the plant a rest, but don't let it dry right out. Feed
every two weeks in the summer and autumn.

Spathiphyllum wallisii (White sails)
A long-term flowering plant producing white sail-like flowers in spring. For the rest of the year the plant makes a good
foliage specimen as it has long shiny deep green leaves. Sometimes the variety 'Mauna Loa' is offered which makes a
slightly larger specimen.

Keep the plant in a temperature of 16°C (60°F) with a
minimum of 13°C (55°F) and provide high humidity. Do not
subject the plant to direct sun although it needs bright light.
During spring and summer keep the compost steadily moist
but be far more sparing with water in autumn and winter. Pot
on annually until the plant is in a large pot and feed fortnightly during spring and summer.

MAY

Dieffenbachia maculata Dumb cane
Dieffenbachias are very popular foliage plants and eventually
make quite large specimens. They have large leaves which
are variegated green and cream or green and creamy yellow.
A number of varieties are available, the most popular being
'Exotica' which is very heavily variegated. A word of warning: the sap of dieffenbachias will cause intense pain and
swelling if it comes in contact with mouth or eyes.

Grow the plant in a warm room with a temperature of 21°C
(70°F) and a minimum at night of 16°C (60°F). High humidity is needed, provided by a gravel tray and by mist spraying
the leaves. Provide good bright light but avoid direct sun.
Keep the compost steadily moist throughout the year and
feed fortnightly in the growing season. Pot on annually until
the plant is in a large pot.

Hydrangea (Pot hydrangea)
Hardy garden hydrangeas are offered as flowering pot plants
in the spring. They are not easy to flower again indoors but

when the display is over they could be planted in the garden. The huge mop-like flower heads may be blue, purple, red, pink or white.

Grow hydrangeas in your coolest room – a suitable temperature range is 10-16°C (50-60°F). The plants need high humidity and like good light (but not direct sun), although it is possible to keep the plants in a shady corner. A lot of water is needed in the spring and summer when the plants are in full growth, together with fortnightly liquid feeding.

Peperomia (Pepper elder)
Very popular small foliage plants. There are several kinds you can buy including *P. obtusifolia* 'Variegata' which has large thick leaves variegated green and cream. Then there are *P. caperata* with deeply crinkled dark green foliage and *P. argyreia* whose leaves are striped with green and silver.

Provide a temperature not lower than 16°C (60°F) and very high humidity. The plants grow well in slight shade and must not be subjected to direct sun. Be careful with watering – if the compost remains very wet the roots may rot. So give water only when the compost is drying out. Feed every two weeks in spring and summer and pot on when the plants are pot-bound as only small pots are needed.

Saintpaulia (African violet)
Probably one of the most popular long-term flowering pot plants but not one of the easiest as it needs very high humidity (try growing it in the bathroom or kitchen) and a steady temperature of 16-18°C (60-65°F). There are many varieties available with flowers in shades of red, pink, purple, blue and white, as well as bicoloured. There are now strains available for lower temperatures (13°C [55°F]), such as the 'Endurance' strain.

Provide really bright light but avoid strong sunshine which can scorch the leaves. Keep the plants in small pots as they have only shallow root systems. The compost should be kept moderately moist from mid-spring to early autumn and much drier for the remainder of the year. It is important to avoid wetting the leaves. In the growing season feed every two weeks. Regularly pick off dead flowers.

Tolmiea menziesii (Pick-a-back plant)

This is a hardy foliage plant with light green heart-shaped leaves which carry tiny plantlets at their bases. These can be used for propagation. An ideal plant for your coolest rooms, it looks particularly attractive when elevated – try growing it in a hanging basket or pot holder.

A suitable temperature range is 7-16°C (45-60°F). A little humidity is appreciated in warmer conditions and the plant can be grown successfully in slight shade. Moderate watering throughout the year is recommended together with fort-nightly liquid feeding in spring and summer.

JUNE

Calceolaria (Slipperwort)

Highly colourful early summer pot plants which are dis-carded after flowering, which lasts for many weeks. The plants have pouched flowers mainly in bright colours (often spotted) like reds, yellows and oranges.

Cool conditions will ensure the flowers last for a long time, an ideal temperature being 10°C (50°F). Provide a little humidity, but do not mist spray the plants, and good light but not direct strong sun. Keep the compost moist at all times but do not bother with feeding.

Cordyline terminalis (Cabbage palm)

Not a true palm, but shaped rather like one, this long-term foliage plant is very popular as a specimen plant. The long broad leaves are bronze-red; but there are several varieties like 'Rededge' with red and green foliage, and 'Tricolor' whose leaves are red, pink and cream. Expect an eventual height of at least 1 m (3 ft).

An ideal temperature is 21°C (70°F) but it can drop to 13-16°C (55-60°F) at night. Provide high humidity, good light but protect from strong sunshine, and water well in the spring and summer but keep the compost only slightly moist in autumn/winter. Feed fortnightly in growing season.

Dracaena deremensis (Dragon lily)

Long-lived popular foliage plants. There are several kinds

available including *D. deremensis* 'Bausei', with green and white striped leaves; *D. d.* 'Warneckii' with similar foliage; and *D. fragrans* and its varieties whose leaves are striped with green and cream or with green and yellow.

Provide a temperature of 21°C (70°F) but this can drop at night to 13°C (55°F). Ensure high humidity at all times, including mist-spraying the leaves, and bright light but avoid strong sunshine. The compost should be kept steadily moist in the growing season but in autumn and winter allow it to become partially dry before giving water. Feed fortnightly in growing season and pot on annually.

Maranta leuconeura (Prayer plant)

A very popular dwarf foliage plant. The leaves turn upwards at night, hence the popular name. The foliage is highly colourful, containing shades of green, purple and blue. There are several varieties with equally colourful leaves like *M.l.* 'Erythrophylla' and *M.l.* 'Massangeana'; and *M.l.* 'Kerchoveana' whose leaves have reddish-brown blotches.

Provide a temperature of 16-21°C (60-70°F), very high humidity and bright light, but shade the plant from strong sunshine. The compost must be kept steadily moist in spring and summer but in autuman and winter allow it to partially dry out between waterings. Pot on annually and feed fortnightly in the growing season.

Nephrolepis exaltata (Sword fern)

A widely grown fern with light, bright green, deeply cut arching fronds or leaves. It looks most spectacular when grown in an elevated container such as a hanging basket or pot holder.

Provide a temperature of 16°C (60°F) and high humidity, including mist spraying of the foliage. This fern likes bright light but not direct sun. The compost should be kept moist all the year round. Feed fortnightly in spring and summer and pot-on only when the plant becomes pot-bound.

Cyclamen flower over a long period in autumn and winter.

Pelargonium domesticum (**Regal pelargonium**)

A popular pot plant which flowers freely in early summer, having blooms in shades of red, pink, purple, white, etc. The plants can be kept for several years but it is best to raise new ones each year from cuttings.

Provide a temperature of 16°C (60°F) in spring and summer but during autumn and winter reduce this to 10°C (50°F). Pelargoniums need dry air and plenty of sunshine. Water well during spring and summer but in autumn/winter the compost should be kept only just moist. Liquid feed every two weeks in the growing season and stand the plants in a sunny spot outside for the summer, after flowering. Pot on in spring using John Innes potting compost.

Tradescantia (**Wandering Jew**)

This must be one of the most popular trailing foliage plants, ideal for hanging baskets or elevated pot holders. One of the best varieties is undoubtedly 'Quicksilver' whose leaves are boldly striped green and silvery white.

A temperature range of 16-21°C (60-70°F) is recommended but at night this can drop to 10°C (50°F). The plants enjoy high humidity and bright light but not direct sun. In spring and summer keep the compost steadily moist but in autumn and winter allow it to partially dry out between waterings. Liquid feed every two weeks in spring and summer and pot on annually. Renew frequently from cuttings as young plants are the most attractive.

Zebrina pendula (**Wandering Jew**)

Similar in a way to tradescantia, this trailer has silver and green banded leaves which are purple on the undersides. Again the plant should ideally be elevated. Cultivation as for tradescantia.

Yucca elephantipes (**Spineless yucca**)

Currently this is a highly popular foliage plant which makes a dramatic specimen plant in a room, especially in a modern setting. It has a thick bare trunk at the top of which it carries a cluster of long erect sword-like leaves.

A temperature range of 13-18°C (55-65°F) is suitable and

the plant needs a fairly dry atmosphere so do not provide any extra humidity. Bright light is essential, including some sunshine. In the spring and summer keep the compost steadily moist but in autumn and winter allow it to partially dry out between waterings. Feed fortnightly in spring and summer. Grow the plant in John Innes potting compost in a clay pot.

JULY

Begonia (Begonia)

Begonias which are grown for their coloured foliage include the ever-popular *Begonia rex* which has multi-coloured leaves (for example market with pink, red, silver, purple and white), and the Iron Cross begonia, *B. masoniana,* with rough green leaves each of which has a bronzy purple cross in the centre.

The ideal temperature for these and other foliage begonias is 21°C (70°F) but it can go down to 16°C (60°F) at night. Very high humidity is required but do not use a mist sprayer on begonias. Diffused light is suitable or slight shade. Water with great care: only when the compost starts to dry out. In winter be even more sparing. Feed fortnightly in spring and summer and move on to a larger pot only when the present one is packed full of roots. Begonias do not like large pots.

Beloperone guttata (Shrimp plant)

A popular shrubby plant which has an incredibly long flowering period, producing long pink and white shrimp-like flowers. It's a good idea to replace older plants regularly with new ones – cuttings root very easily.

Provide a temperature between 16 and 21°C (60 and 70°F); in winter 10°C (50°F). Ensure moderate humidity and bright light but shade the plant from very strong scorching sun. Keep well watered when in full growth and only very slightly moist during the winter rest period. A weekly feed is appreciated in spring and summer. Pot on annually and use John Innes potting compost. Large plants can be pruned back by half in winter.

The winter cherry, *Solanum capsicastrum*, is a popular, short-term, pot plant.

Caladium bicolor (**Angel's wings**)

This is a very delicate tropical foliage plant which will only grow in the conditions described below. It is offered in the summer and the leaves die down in autumn. These are paper-thin and generally multicoloured. Colours include red, pink, white and green.

It is essential to provide a temperature of at least 18°C (65°F) during the spring and summer. The plant dies back and rests over winter when it should be kept in a temperature of 13°C (55°F). Humidity must be as high as you can possibly provide during the growing season. Leaves must certainly be sprayed daily with tepid water. Provide bright light but not direct sun. In spring and summer the compost should be kept steadily moist but it should be dried off for the winter. Weekly feeds in the growing season will help to keep the plant happy. In early spring repot the plant into fresh compost, resume watering and increase the temperature.

Coleus (Flame nettle)

Popular foliage plants which are generally discarded at the end of the season as young plants are the most attractive. The leaves come in many brilliant colour combinations.

Provide a temperature of about 16°C (60°F). High humidity is necessary together with maximum light but shade the plants from direct sun. The compost must be kept steadily moist throughout the spring and summer, when fortnightly feeds can also be given.

Hypoestes phyllostachya (Polka dot plant)

This is a fairly new foliage plant which is small and bushy, the leaves being heavily spotted and splashed with pink.

Provide a temperature range of 13-18°C (55-65°F), high humidity and bright light but beware of stong scorching sunshine. The compost should be allowed to dry out partially between waterings.

Feed fortnightly in spring and summer. Pot on plants annually – or more often if necessary.

Impatiens (Busy Lizzie)

These pot plants flower their heads off throughout the summer and well into autumn. It is best to discard them in the autumn – they can be replaced with new ones easily enough by taking cuttings. Flowers come in many brilliant colours – reds, oranges, pinks, white, etc. There are double-flowered varieties, too.

A temperature of 21°C (70°F) is recommended but it can drop at night to as low as 13°C (55°F). High humidity is needed together with bright light, including some sunshine, but beware of hot scorching sun. Water generously in spring and summer but keep the plants only barely moist in autumn/winter. Feed every two weeks and pot on regularly as required. Remove dead flowers.

Streptocarpus (Cape primrose)

Flowering pot plants which can be kept for some years. They bloom all summer and into autumn. The trumpet-shaped blooms may be in shades of blue, pink, red, purple or white.

Maintain a temperature of 16-18°C (60-65°F), with 10°C

(50°F) over the winter rest period. Moderate humidity is recommended during the growing season and good light, but do protect the plants from strong sunshine. The compost must be kept steadily moist during the growing season, when fortnightly feeds should be given. The compost should be kept on the dry side in winter. Pick off dead blooms to encourage more to follow.

AUGUST

Aechmea fasciata (Urn plant)
A foliage and flowering plant – and very popular. It forms a tall rosette of leaves which are silvery green and form a water-holding vase which should be kept filled with fresh water. The flower head consists of a bright pink cluster of leaves (bracts) through which appear lilac or blue flowers.

Provide a temperature of 16°C (60°F) and a minimum of 10°C (50°F) at night. High humidity is needed in warm conditions plus bright light but not direct sun. The compost should be kept reasonably moist all through the year. Feed monthly in spring and summer. Only pot on the plant when pot-bound, using the next size of pot. A peat-based compost is preferred.

Calathea makoyana (Peacock plant)
A long-lived foliage plant with quite large leaves, these being boldly marked with various shades of green, plus silver, and they're purple below.

Ensure a temperature range of 16-21°C (60-70°F) with a minimum of 10°C (50°F), high humidity and light shade. Water well in spring and summer but moderately in autumn and winter. Feed fortnightly when in full growth and pot on in spring if necessary.

Campanula isophylla (Bellflower)
An almost hardy trailing plant, ideal for your coolest rooms, which can be kept for several years. The bell-shaped flowers are blue but there is also a white variety. Try growing it in a hanging basket or other elevated container.

It needs a temperature around 10-16°C (50-60°F) – certainly no higher. Provide a little humidity in warm conditions and good light but not hot sun. In the growing season plenty of water is needed but the compost should be kept only slightly moist in winter. Feed fortnightly during the growing season and pick off dead flowers regularly. After flowering (some time in autumn) cut back the stems almost to compost level. Keep the plant cool in winter. Propagate plants regularly from cuttings as young specimens flower best.

Ficus (Rubber plants and figs)

The rubber plant, *Ficus elastica* 'Decora', is found in almost every home. It makes a handsome large specimen plant with its large, leathery, deep green glossy leaves. Also very popular is the weeping fig, *Ficus benjamina,* which has arching branches carrying small rubber-plant-like leaves.

A temperature of 16-21°C (60-70°F) is needed together with high humidity. Provide good light but not direct sun. The compost must be kept moist in spring and summer but allow it to dry out partially between waterings in autumn and winter. Feed fortnightly in spring and summer and pot on annually until the plants are in large pots.

Monstera deliciosa (Swiss cheese plant)

As popular as the rubber plant and making an equally large dramatic specimen with its huge deeply cut and perforated leaves. It is a climbing plant best supported with one of the moss poles which you can buy in garden centres. Keep the moss moist.

The recommended temperature is 16-21°C (60-70°F) with a minimum of 10°C (50°F). Provide high humidity. The plant grows in good light (not direct sun) to light shade. Water generously in spring and summer but keep the compost only barely moist in autumn and winter. Feed fortnightly during the growing season and pot on annually until the plant is in a large pot.

Philodendron (Philodendron)

Many of these foliage plants are similar in habit to the Swiss cheese plant, most of them being climbers and best trained up moss poles. Some popular kinds are *P. angustisectum* (also known as *P. elegans*) with deeply cut leaves; *P. erubescens* with big arrow-shaped leaves; *P. scandens* with small heart-shaped leaves; and *P.* 'Burgundy' whose leaves are shield-shaped and red on the undersides.

Ideal temperature is 21°C (70°F) with a minimum at night of 16°C (60°F). High humidity is essential. Plants can be grown in shady areas; avoid direct sun. In spring and summer keep the compost steadily moist but in autumn and winter allow it to dry out partially between waterings. When plants are in full growth feed every two weeks. Pot on annually until plants are in large pots.

Scindapsus aureus (Devil's ivy)
A climbing foliage plant with green and yellow variegated heart-shaped leaves. Grow it up a moss pole.

The ideal temperature is 21°C (70°F) and it should not drop below 16°C (60°F). Ensure high humidity and good

The bracts of poinsettias last for many months and then the plants are best discarded.

light (but avoid strong sun). The plant will, however, survive in quite a dark corner if necessary. Do not overwater the devil's ivy: the compost should be kept only slightly moist in spring and summer, while in autumn and winter give water only when it has virtually dried out. Feed fortnightly in spring and summer and pot on annually until a large pot is reached.

SEPTEMBER

Cissus rhombifolia (Grape ivy)
A popular, vigorous, very tough climber with deep green lobed leaves.

A good temperature to maintain is 16°C (60°F) but the plant will survive if it drops as low as 4.5°C (40°F). Ensure moderate humidity in warm conditions – the plant enjoys having its leaves mist sprayed. The plant can be grown in deep shade if necessary, or in bright light but not very strong sunshine. To avoid risking root rot water the plant only when the compost has virtually dried out. Feed fortnightly in spring and summer and pot on annually. The plant can be cut back if it becomes too tall.

Sansevieria trifasciata 'Laurentii' (Mother-in-law's tongue)
Another very tough and adaptable foliage plant, with erect sword-like leaves banded greyish green and boldly edged with yellow. Suitable for any room in the house.

The ideal temperature is 16-21°C (60-70°F) with a minimum of 10°C (50°F). A dry atmosphere is needed and light conditions can vary from sunshine to shade. Best results, though, in bright conditions. Do not overwater: wait until the compost becomes dry. Monthly feeding should be carried out in spring and summer. Pot on the plant only when it is pot-bound as it does not like too large a pot.

OCTOBER

Capsicum annuum (Ornamental pepper)
A short-term pot plant which produces cone-shaped orange

or red fruits in autumn and winter. It becomes available from this time of year onwards.

Grow it in a cool room with a temperature of around 10°C (50°F). It likes dry air and good bright light. Keep the compost steadily moist.

Hedera (**Ivy**)

Tough, hardy, climbing or trailing foliage plants for cool rooms. The varieties of the common ivy, *Hedera helix*, have plain green or variegated leaves. Then there's the large-leaved cream and green variegated Canary Island ivy, *H. canariensis* 'Variegata', extremely popular as a houseplant.

Although lower temperatures are acceptable, try to provide 10-16°C (50-60°F). Ivies do not mind draughty places. Moderate humidity is enjoyed including mist-spraying the leaves. Variegated ivies need bright light (but not direct sun) while the plain green kinds will take fairly dark corners. In spring and summer the compost should be kept steadily moist but be very sparing with water in autumn and winter when you should wait until the compost has almost dried out. Feed fortnightly in spring and summer and pot on annually.

NOVEMBER

Chrysanthemum (**Dwarf pot chrysanthemum**)

Dwarf pot chrysanthemums can be bought in flower all the year round but what better time to buy than in the autumn – the chrysanthemum's 'real' season. They come in a wide range of colours including yellow, pink and red and are discarded after flowering.

Keep the plants in a cool room where the blooms will last for many weeks. The temperature can be as low as 5°C (40°F). Very slight humidity is recommended in warm weather. Provide maximum light. The compost should be kept steadily moist. Don't bother with feeding but remove dead flowers.

Cyclamen (**Florist's cyclamen**)

Plants are available in autumn and winter and they flower over a very long period. Colours include shades of red and pink and also white. Miniature cyclamen with scented flowers are becoming very popular as are those with silver-marbled foliage. Although plants can be kept for many years a lot of people discard them after flowering.

Ideal for a coolish room – aim for 13-16°C (55-60°F). Moderate humidity is required but do not spray plants. Provide maximum light. Water only when the compost is becoming dry but do avoid wetting the centre of the plant or leaf and flower stems may rot. Remove dead flowers and leaves.

Solanum capsicastrum (Winter cherry)
This popular short-term pot plant produces orange or red berries during autumn and winter.

Provide a temperature of 13-16°C (55-60°F), moderate humidity (plants can be sprayed daily) and maximum light. The compost should be kept moist. No need to feed.

DECEMBER

Euphorbia pulcherrima (Poinsettia)
Extremely popular at Christmas time, plants produce large colourful 'bracts' (modified leaves) in red, pink or cream. They are treated as temporary plants and discarded after flowering as it is extremely difficult to get the plants to produce bracts again in normal room conditions.

Provide a temperature of 16°C (60°F), slight humidity and bright light. Be careful with watering – allow the compost to dry out partially between waterings. No need to feed.

Hyacinthus (Hyacinth)
Hyacinths can be forced to flower at Christmas time but you must buy specially treated bulbs and plant them in early autumn. It is also possible to buy bulbs already potted and coming into flower.

If you want to plant your own put three bulbs in a 15 cm (6 in) bulb bowl, using bulb fibre and leaving the tops of the bulbs exposed. Keep the fibre moist at all times. Keep the bulbs as cool as possible and in complete darkness. When shoots are about 5 cm (2 in) high transfer to a temperature of 10°C (50°F). Increase to 16°C (60°F) when flower buds are visible. Maximum light is necessary once the bulbs come out of complete darkness. The bulbs can be planted in the garden after flowering.

Narcissus (Daffodils)
Specially prepared bulbs will flower in time for Christmas if treated as for hyacinths. It is possible to buy bulbs already potted and coming into flower.

Rhododendron (Azalea)
Dwarf evergreen azaleas are very popular around Christmas time and can be kept for many years. They come in a wide range of colours including shades of red, pink, purple, mauve and also white.

Azaleas should be kept in a cool room as they are almost hardy: 13-16°C (55-60°F) is a suitable temperature range. Provide high humidity and bright light but avoid sunshine. The compost must be kept steadily moist all year round. Water with rainwater or 'soft' (lime-free) tap water. Feed fortnightly in spring and summer. Pot on as necessary in spring using ericaceous (lime-free) compost. The plant should be stood out of doors in a shady spot for the summer.

Schlumbergera × buckleyi (Christmas cactus)
One can never guarantee that this plant will flower at Christmas time: sometimes it does, sometimes it flowers in the New Year. It bears magenta or deep pink blooms. When flower buds start to form avoid moving or turning the plant or they will drop off.

Ensure a minimum temperature in autumn and winter of 10°C (50°F) and at least 18°C (65°F) for the rest of the year. Provide high humidity when conditions are warm, far less in cooler conditions. Ensure bright light but shade the plants from sun during the spring and summer. Christmas cacti like fresh air and should be watered all year round (unlike other cacti) but wait until the compost has partially dried out. Pot on as required, using peat-based potting compost. Feed fortnightly during spring and summer.

The Christmas cactus, *Schlumbergera × buckleyi*, may flower during or after the festive season.